M000303826

WITHDRAWN
BY
JEFFERSON COUNTY PUBLIC LIBRARY
Lakewood, CO

Praise for *Getting It to Stick*

Historically, we have never had more access to God's word, scholarly input and biblical knowledge, yet we are fighting the challenge of Biblical illiteracy around the nation. In her simple devotional, Debbie Bailey creatively addresses every parent's desire to help teach their children how to integrate Life and Faith. Topically, she addresses themes that are both cultural and current and then deftly fosters a conversation that leads to scripture. Starting with the premise that faith is not meant to live in isolation *Getting It to Stick* promotes the integration of life and faith in a clear, compelling and do-able way! There is an elegance in its simplicity that should make every parent grateful!

KEN TANKERSLEY, Senior Vice President,
Young Life Global Innovation and Training

With all of the noise filling teenagers heads through social media it is hard for parents to know how to help teenagers not only hear but believe God's truths for their lives. In her book Getting It To Stick, Debbie Bailey offers practical yet profound tips for ways to help keep our kids rooted in the Word of God.

REV. JENNY TREES, Pastor of Spiritual Formation
and Spiritual Director, Walnut Creek, CA

Getting It to Stick is a wonderfully practical and creative resource to get our kids and grandkids into God's Word. It will change their lives and yours. Highly recommended!

MARLENE BAGNULL, Author, Speaker, Editor,
Publisher Ampelos Press, Director of Write His Answer Ministries

Finally, a family devotion that provides a pastoral resource for us parents who want a quick and simple plan to have scripture be the center of our kid's day. I am so glad there are people out there like Debbie, who can thoughtfully organize scripture themes so I can focus on being pastoral with my children and pray for them.

WENDY EVERTS, author of
The Challenge (A Christian novel for teens)

In *Getting It To Stick*, Debbie Bailey meets the millennia-old mandate to instill an understanding and appreciation for God and His Word in our priceless kids' hearts with a short, sweet, unique twist. If you're a believing parent or grandparent, you'll be so glad you picked up this book!

KIM WOODARD OSTERHOLZER, author of
A Midwife in Amish Country, Celebrating God's Gift of Life

This devotional is a refreshing look and take on today's struggles. You will find each chapter relevant and applicable to everyday life not only with your teenager but also with yourself!

AMIE PILLER, Mother of Six and
Director of Administrative Assistants, Jubilee Community Church

This is a prayer guide for our children as well as for us. What a way to start each day! The seeds that will be planted for God's Kingdom through this book will be IMPACTFUL!

"MOMMA J" - JUDY HAZELWOOD
Evangelist and Mother

DEBBIE BAILEY

A Parent's Devotional to Incorporate
God's Word Into the Life of Your Teen

KINGDOM
PUBLISHING

Getting It To Stick
Copyright © 2018 Debbie Bailey

ISBN 978-1-7322879-1-4 (hardcover)
ISBN 978-1-7322879-2-1 (ebook)

Scriptures taken from the Holy Bible, New International Version®, NIV®. Copyright © 1973, 1978, 1984, 2011 by Biblica, Inc.™ Used by permission of Zondervan. All rights reserved worldwide. www.zondervan.com The "NIV" and "New International Version" are trademarks registered in the United States Patent and Trademark Office by Biblica, Inc.™

Cover Design: Tracy Fagan
Cover Photograph: James SD Photography

All rights reserved.
No part of this publication may be reproduced in any form without written permission from Kingdom Publishing, PO Box 653, Parker, Colorado 80134

Publisher's Cataloging-in-Publication data

Names: Bailey, Debbie Renee, author.
Title: Getting it to stick : A parent's devotional to incorporate God's Word into the life of your teen / Debbie Bailey.
Description: First original edition. | Also available as an ebook. | Parker [Colorado] : Kingdom Publishing, 2018.
Identifiers: ISBN 978-1-7322879-1-4
Subjects: LCSH: Devotional exercises. | Families--Prayers and devotions.
BISAC: RELIGION / Christian Life / Devotional.
Classification: LCC BV4800 2018 | DDC 242.2–dc22

Dedication

This book is dedicated to my husband, Thompson, and my four children, Christie, Connor, Blake and Cam. Thank you for your love and support. I love you to the moon and back.

To my mom, Vickie, my mother-n-law, Raine, and my dear friend, Wendy Baker. Thank you for encouraging me to write and for believing in me. I also want to thank Cindy Lambert for helping me with my proposal and giving me great wisdom for this book.

I want to thank Beatrice Bruno and Kim Amen for working diligently on editing my book. You are both a blessing.

To Tracy Fagan at Kingdom Publishing. Thank you for reaching out and making this all happen. I am truly grateful.

Table of Contents

Introduction

*I have hidden your word in my heart that
I might not sin against you.*
Psalm 119:11

When my kids were young, I wanted the Word of God hidden in their little hearts. So I began to search for the best way to accomplish this. I have to say that I found it a harder task than I expected. Church is wonderful, but one day a week is not enough. They needed the Word on a daily basis.

I discovered AWANA, an awesome program where children learn, practice, and memorize God's word. We began the program, but it was a big commitment that we did not follow through on. Next, I bought them each a Bible and put it by their bedsides. You know the ones with the soccer ball and basketball covers, thinking these boy themes would entice them to open the Bible and read. Nope. They pretty much sat there.

I thought about how the Bible can be overwhelming and hard to understand, even for many adults. Why would it be any different for children and teens? So I went out and bought devotional books for teens. I read them aloud to my boys before bed. The devotional explained a verse, gave a story, and ended with a prayer. Even that seemed long for my boys who quickly lost interest. As I finished reading the written prayer, one would say, "Amen. Okay, Mom, tomorrow can we go to the park after school?"

"Did you hear the devotional I just read?"

"Yeah, it talked about God and being good."

"What else?"

Shrug.

After a few weeks of this, I felt frustrated. *Lord, Your Word is important. Hopefully a little bit is sinking in from these devotionals. What should I do?*

I went to the boys' room and sat on a bed, lifting the devotional from the nightstand. They were probably still worth reading, but it wasn't enough. *Lord, I don't want learning Your Word to be a chore. How can I feed them every day?*

I believed Proverbs 22:6 which says, *Start children off on the way they should go, and even when they are old they will not turn from it.* But how? I had tried the traditional methods that hadn't worked for our family.

I put down the devotional book and picked up the Bible with the basketballs on the cover and opened it. It did look overwhelming. How could I make scripture a part of their hearts and lives while keeping it short and sweet, to the point? How could I give the Word to them in a way that they would understand? I had seen how understanding Him and His ways, hearing the Word, speaking the Word, and living the Word changes lives! I desperately wanted this for my children.

I turned the pages to Romans 10:17. *Consequently, faith comes from hearing the message, and the message is heard through the word about Christ.*

And then an idea came to me, surely placed there by the Holy Spirit.

I know I'm not the only one who struggles with this problem. All Christian parents want their teens to know the Word of God and have it infiltrate their lives in meaningful ways. However, because many families live such busy lifestyles today, parents like me feel at a loss to find a simple solution for presenting God's Word in such a way that it captures the attention of their teens. On a day-to-day basis, we get caught up "in the world" and often put God on the back burner. But the Word is the key to abundance, peace, knowledge, rest, and perseverance.

The unfolding of your words gives light; it gives understanding to the simple. Psalm 119:130

Getting It to Stick provides a simple way for busy, overwhelmed parents and grandparents to share God's Word with their children and grandchildren in ways they will easily notice and comprehend so that the Word can come alive in their hearts.

Two years ago, I put into practice the idea that came to me—I have taken God's Word and written those truths on my kids' bathroom mirrors. I take a verse, theme, truth, or promise and write it in Expo dry erase marker (it comes off with glass cleaner). I write a new one every week. I found that if I kept it on too long, it just became background and my boys started to ignore it. I write it in different ways, on different parts of the mirror; on the top, next on the bottom, on the side, in a bubble with a cute character next to it. They see it, read it, and I add the secret ingredient which is to pray it will sink into their hearts.

For the word of the LORD is right and true; He is faithful in all He does. Psalm 33:4

This little book presents a simple encouraging sentence for each key Bible verse. A parent can post this sentence where their teen will quickly and easily see it, read it, and be encouraged to believe it and live it. Even more, it provides creative ideas on how, when, and where these can be posted, along with simple ideas to encourage discussions of how God's truths can infiltrate their lives in practical ways. Each entry ends with a prayer for the parent. Feel free to read the prayer provided over your tween/teen, or write or pray your own prayer related to this week's topic. A journal page is included for written prayers for your children. This will be a great tool to cover them in prayer. Imagine what it would be like to have that prayer journal as a keepsake for them when they are older.

Blessed rather are those who hear the word of God and obey it.
Luke 11:28

Post it, See it, Read it, Believe it, Live it!

Chapter 1
Speak Life

I started with this subject because this is what my whole teen devotional is about. I want our teens to speak life into themselves and into their situations. What does it mean to speak life? It means to speak God's Word, to speak God's truths, to speak God's promises. Our tongues are a means for either good or bad. God knows His Word is powerful and He knows His Words can heal, encourage, restore, bless, strengthen, guide, protect, correct, and direct us. Before the circumstance or the problem is resolved, we need to teach our children that God will deliver them according to His Word. It takes faith to see the invisible and call it forth. Jesus always spoke the good that He wanted to see happen. Let's help our teens speak life!

Each week, write the Post It thought on a sticky note and post it on your teen(s) bathroom mirror. This will be one of the first things they see in the morning. We have to help our children see that God's Word has power.

WEEK 1

> May the words out of my mouth come from You, Lord.
>
> Your words are truth.
>
> They encourage, strengthen, protect, and heal me.

Scripture:

The mouth of the righteous is a fountain of life.
Proverbs 10:11

Conversation Starters

- Why is it good to know the Bible and read God's Word?
- Is all of God's Word truth?

The SECRET Ingredient of Prayer:

Dear Lord, Thank You for helping my child/children to delight in Your Word. The more they delight in It, the more they will speak It. I pray they learn to speak Your Word into their situations instead of focusing on lies. Ashes can be turned into beauty by what they speak. Thank You that they will truly understand Your truth. In Jesus' name, Amen.

Week 1 Observations ~ Thoughts ~ Feelings ~ Prayers

....

....

....

....

....

....

....

....

....

....

....

....

....

....

....

....

....

....

....

WEEK 2

> My words have power.
> They can either hurt or help me and my family and friends.
> I will choose to speak encouraging words.

Scripture:

From the fruit of their mouth a person's stomach is filled; with the harvest of their lips they are satisfied. The tongue has the power of life and death, and those who love it will eat its fruit.

Proverbs 18:20 – 21

Conversation Starters

- What does it mean to speak life and death?

- How can our words hurt us and those we love?

The SECRET Ingredient of Prayer:

Father in Heaven, thank You for Your Words. May my child/children learn Your truths and speak life into their situations. Even when they are feeling down, not good enough, or they are physically sick, may they realize Your Words have power and they bring hope and healing. Your truths trump the devil's lies. Your truth gives life to our mortal bodies. Thank You for penetrating this into their hearts and minds. In Jesus' name, Amen.

Week 2 Observations ~ Thoughts ~ Feelings ~ Prayers

....

....

....

....

....

....

....

....

....

....

....

....

....

....

....

....

....

....

WEEK 3

Lord, help me to keep my mouth from negative talk.

I want to experience an amazing life and feed myself and others with joy!

Scripture:

*Those who guard their mouths and their tongues
keep themselves from calamity.*
Proverbs 21:23

Conversation Starters

- Do your words really matter and why?

- Can we really destroy ourselves by speaking negatively?

The SECRET Ingredient of Prayer:

Dear Heavenly Father, we are who You say we are because Your Word is truth. Help my child/children to speak life-giving words about themselves and others. Give them the desire to obey Your commands. Your Words are priceless! Every word You spoke and every word we speak that is from You is valuable. Help my child/children truly understand the power of what they say and help them to be more aware of what they are even thinking. Our lives can truly become transformed when we have faith in You. Thank You, Father. In Jesus' name I pray, Amen.

Week 3 Observations ~ Thoughts ~ Feelings ~ Prayers

WEEK 4

> I will try my best to build others up. If I don't have anything nice to say, I won't say it at all. when I speak negatively about someone, it just makes me look bad and insecure. May I be a positive force in this hurting world.

Scripture:

Do not let any unwholesome talk come out of your mouths, but only what is helpful for building others up according to their needs, that it may benefit those who listen.

Ephesians 4:29

Conversation Starters

- Why does speaking negatively about others make ourselves look bad?

- Why do we need to be a positive force instead of just stating the obvious?

The SECRET Ingredient of Prayer:

Thank You again, Father, for helping my child/children be that positive force in this hurting world. Help them to lift people up and not bring them down. Encourage them to obey Your nudges to speak life into someone. Please help them hold their tongue when they want to lash out. We can't do this without You. Continue to give them direction and wisdom with their thoughts and voice. In Jesus' name, Amen.

Week 4 Observations ~ Thoughts ~ Feelings ~ Prayers

....

....

....

....

....

....

....

....

....

....

....

....

....

....

....

....

....

....

Observations ~ Thoughts ~ Feelings ~ Prayers

....

....

....

....

....

....

....

....

....

....

....

....

....

....

....

....

....

....
....
....
....
....
....
....
....
....
....
....
....
....
....
....
....
....
....
....

Chapter 2

Anxiety

For teens, anxiety is a normal reaction to the stressful situations they experience. Teens have tests that they take, they go on dates, compete in sports, meet new people, and they will encounter issues with family members or friends. It is important for teens to recognize their emotions and admit that a situation can be stressful so they are prepared to deal with it. Anxiety can cause a teen to perform poorly in school, engage in substance abuse, or miss out on important social experiences. God's Word has very encouraging words for anxiety. Truly knowing His Word can only give them the peace they need.

Put the post-it notes on their night stand, near their beds. Hopefully, they are waking up to God's Word and not a text. I highly recommend that you encourage your children not to sleep with their phones. Personally I don't think it is safe for their developing brains. Additionally, I also know many children lose precious sleep because they stay up late wasting time on their phones. Make God's wisdom the first thing they wake up to.

WEEK 1

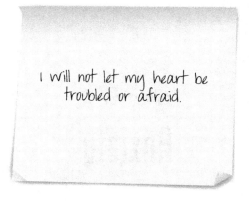

I will not let my heart be troubled or afraid.

Scripture:

Peace I leave with you; my peace I give you.
I do not give to you as the world gives.
Do not let your hearts be troubled and do not be afraid.
John 14:27

Conversation Starters

- What sorts of ways can God help you with a situation you may have with a friend?
- How can you trust God's Word?

The SECRET Ingredient of Prayer:

Dear Father God, I thank You for Your Word and Its truth. I thank You that no matter what anxieties my son/daughter may have through past experiences, they will remember what You have done for them. I thank You that Your Word will come alive for them and that You will hear and answer them when they pray. In Jesus' name, Amen.

Week 1 Observations ~ Thoughts ~ Feelings ~ Prayers

....

....

....

....

....

....

....

....

....

....

....

....

....

....

....

....

....

WEEK 2

> I will not allow myself to worry. I will recognize that God is working behind the scenes, even when I cannot see external evidence right away.

Scripture:

Therefore do not worry about tomorrow, for tomorrow will worry about itself. Each day has enough trouble of its own.
Matthew 6:34

Conversation Starters

- What does God mean when He says do not worry? Does worry help our situation?

- Parents, share a time when you were concerned about a situation but handed it to God. What was the outcome?

The SECRET Ingredient of Prayer:

Dear Heavenly Father, it is hard not to worry, even for me. But You have so graciously taught me to lean on You. Thank You for also teaching my son/daughter to lean on You. Thank You that they will be released from the bondage of worry. Thank You that they will know that you are working behind the scenes on their behalf. Let them feel Your peace. In Jesus' name, Amen.

Week 2 Observations ~ Thoughts ~ Feelings ~ Prayers

....

....

....

....

....

....

....

....

....

....

....

....

....

....

....

....

....

....

WEEK 3

God, I believe at the right time, You will change things in my favor.

Scripture:

Have I not commanded you? Be strong and courageous.
Do not be afraid; do not be discouraged,
for the LORD your God will be with you wherever you go.
Joshua 1:9

Conversation Starters

- How do you be still and trust God when you have an argument with a friend?
- Do you pray when you have a test or are trying out for a sport?

The SECRET Ingredient of Prayer:

Dear Father God, it's hard even for me to hand over everything to You. Thank You for being with my son/daughter in their low times. Whether it's a disagreement with a friend, a test they are anxious about, or even whether or not they will make a sports team, thank You that they will truly know You care and You have their back. I pray that they will be encouraged with the peace they feel after they pray. Thank You Father. In Jesus' name. Amen.

Week 3 Observations ~ Thoughts ~ Feelings ~ Prayers

....

....

....

....

....

....

....

....

....

....

....

....

....

....

....

....

....

....

WEEK 4

> I have to line up the truth with God's word and not with my circumstances.

Scripture:

Sanctify them by the truth; your word is truth.
John 17:17

Conversation Starters

- Why is it bad to focus on our circumstances?
- When you read God's truth about a situation, do you change your mind and act accordingly or do you let the circumstance override His word?

The SECRET Ingredient of Prayer:

Dear Lord, please help my son/daughter to focus on Your truth and not their circumstance. Give them the desire to want and believe Your Word. You said in Luke 11:9-10, *"So I say to you: Ask and it will be given to you; seek and you will find; knock and the door will be opened to you. For everyone who asks receives; the one who seeks finds; and to the one who knocks, the door will be opened."* Thank You that my child/children will have a passion for Your Word and know that these circumstances will pass. And thank You that they will trust in what You have to say. In Jesus' name I pray, Amen.

Week 4 Observations ~ Thoughts ~ Feelings ~ Prayers

....

....

....

....

....

....

....

....

....

....

....

....

....

....

....

....

....

....

Observations ~ Thoughts ~ Feelings ~ Prayers

....

....

....

....

....

....

....

....

....

....

....

....

....

....

....

....

....
....
....
....
....
....
....
....
....
....
....
....
....
....
....
....
....
....
....

Getting It to Stick

Chapter 3

Conflict

Conflict comes in all sorts of ways in a teen's life. Conflict is the result of perceived or actual differences or incompatibilities. The most important thing I wanted to teach my children about conflict was how to handle it. There is a right way and there is a wrong way. There is God's way and there is our way. Generally, our way is to make sure we are heard, we are right, and we are not perceived as wrong. But God has precious wisdom for those dealing with conflict, and it sure beats our approach.

Put the post-it note in their back pack. However, I would also write it on the mirror of their bathroom as well. Again, I stress that they must see it daily. It will sink in, even if we don't think it is. Do not get discouraged. What you are doing is a wonderful thing. You may experience them not approaching a conflict the way you think they should, but in time, they will. As adults, we do not always handle things the way we should, so be patient with your teens.

WEEK 1

> It is better to speak kindly, that is when I really win. Thank You, Father, for helping me with my tongue.

Scripture:

There is one who speaks rashly like the thrusts of a sword but the tongue of the wise brings healing.

Proverbs 12:18

Conversation Starters

- What conflict have you been involved in lately, sports, girlfriends, guy friends, teachers, and how have you handled it?
- Why does God ask us to speak kindly to others even when we are upset?

The SECRET Ingredient of Prayer:

Dear Heavenly Father, I thank You for your encouragement for all of us. Thank You for simply reminding my child/children to hold their tongue, to speak life into their conflict and not death. In Jesus' name, Amen.

Week 1 Observations ~ Thoughts ~ Feelings ~ Prayers

....

....

....

....

....

....

....

....

....

....

....

....

....

....

....

....

....

....

WEEK 2

I will be quick to listen and slow to speak. Help me, Lord to control my anger.

Scripture:

My dear brothers and sisters, take note of this: Everyone should be quick to listen, slow to speak and slow to become angry.
James 1:19

Conversation Starters

- Why is it important to listen first?
- When you're really upset, what should you do first before you go to the person hurting you?

The SECRET Ingredient of Prayer:

Father God, thank You so much for helping us all to listen and to remember that lashing out hinders us. This is very challenging, especially when we know or feel we are right about the situation. Help our child/ children learn that when they do listen and are slow to speak, they will be free from losing the real battle which is acting unwisely. In Jesus' name we pray, Amen.

Week 2 Observations ~ Thoughts ~ Feelings ~ Prayers

....

....

....

....

....

....

....

....

....

....

....

....

....

....

....

....

....

....

....

WEEK 3

> I will not repay evil with evil. I need to repay evil with a blessing, because I will inherit a blessing. I need to seek peace!

Scripture:

Finally, all of you, be like-minded, be sympathetic, love one another, be compassionate and humble. Do not repay evil with evil or insult with insult. On the contrary, repay evil with blessing, because to this you were called so that you may inherit a blessing. For, "Whoever would love life and see good days must keep their tongue from evil and their lips from deceitful speech. They must turn from evil and do good; they must seek peace and pursue it.

1 Peter 3:8-11

Conversation Starters

- Why is it not good to repay evil for evil?
- Whose job is it to repay evil for evil?

The SECRET Ingredient of Prayer:

Lord, help my child/children to remember that it is Your job to repay evil not theirs. Remind them that they win in the end for holding their tongue and for doing the right thing. Lord, this is very hard for all of us. Thank You that through Jesus, we have all the power to succeed in this area. We love You. In Jesus' name we pray, Amen

Week 3 Observations ~ Thoughts ~ Feelings ~ Prayers

....

....

....

....

....

....

....

....

....

....

....

....

....

....

....

....

....

....

....

WEEK 4

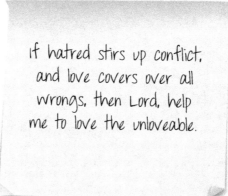

If hatred stirs up conflict, and love covers over all wrongs, then Lord, help me to love the unloveable.

Scripture:

Hatred stirs up conflict, but love covers over all wrongs.
Proverbs 10:12

Conversation Starters

- How do I love someone who has hurt me?
- How does hatred stir up conflict?

The SECRET Ingredient of Prayer:

Father, thank You for speaking wisdom to us. It's hard to deal with people who are unkind to us. Help us to remember that You forgave and continue to forgive us. Please help my child/children realize they are not perfect and that other people need grace, too. Let us be released from the hate that comes our way. In Jesus' name, Amen.

Week 4 Observations ~ Thoughts ~ Feelings ~ Prayers

....

....

....

....

....

....

....

....

....

....

....

....

....

....

....

....

....

....

Observations ~ Thoughts ~ Feelings ~ Prayers

....

....

....

....

....

....

....

....

....

....

....

....

....

....

....

....

....

....

....

....

....

....

....

....

....

....

....

....

....

....

....

....

....

....

....

Chapter 4

Sex

This is a hard subject to tackle. "Everyone is doing it." So they say. What happened to abstinence? For me, the best thing I could do was teach my children what God says about sex, allowing them to make up their own minds about it. We did when we were teenagers. It is so important to teach them to have a plan, or an escape, or never to get into a situation that may be too hard to get out of. The consequences are scary. But sometimes in the moment, they don't recall what they were taught. Not only is it important to teach them how valuable they are, but also how special sex is with your spouse. And then, we should also show them how complicated it is with just a boyfriend/girlfriend.

Place the post-it note on their closet door, where they see it every day. Don't be afraid to have these conversations. The world is talking to your kids about sex daily. This is your opportunity to give them God's perspective on this topic.

WEEK 1

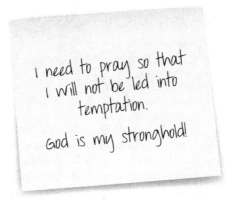

I need to pray so that I will not be led into temptation.

God is my stronghold!

Scripture:

"Watch and pray so that you will not fall into temptation. The spirit is willing, but the flesh is weak."
Matthew 26:41

Conversation Starters

- What will prayer do when we are faced with temptation?
- Why does the Bible say our body is weak? In what ways?

The SECRET Ingredient of Prayer:

Dear Heavenly Father, I just lift my child/children up to You. I know it is so hard to follow the Spirit over the flesh. I pray, in the name of Jesus, that You will give them the desire to follow Your ways. Thank You Father. In Jesus' name I pray, Amen.

Week 1 Observations ~ Thoughts ~ Feelings ~ Prayers

....

....

....

....

....

....

....

....

....

....

....

....

....

....

....

....

....

....

WEEK 2

> I have nothing to prove to anyone. In the end, I answer to my Father in Heaven. Lord, help me refrain from temptation and to know how valuable I am. May I not lower my standards for anyone.

Scripture:

Don't you know that you yourselves are God's temple and that God's Spirit dwells in your midst?

1 Corinthians 3:16

Conversation Starters

- What does it mean that we are God's temple?
- If we don't feel valuable, how do we know we are?

The SECRET Ingredient of Prayer:

Thank You, Father God, that You have our teens in the palm of Your hand. It's not easy out there but they are Yours. I ask in Jesus' name that You give them discernment, protection, and peace about doing things Your way. In Jesus' name I pray, Amen.

Week 2 Observations ~ Thoughts ~ Feelings ~ Prayers

....

....

....

....

....

....

....

....

....

....

....

....

....

....

....

....

....

....

WEEK 3

> Lord, You know I am not perfect and I thank You for do-overs in my life. Thank You that through Christ I am forgiven.

Scripture:

If we confess our sins, He is faithful and just and will forgive us our sins and purify us from all unrighteousness.
1 John 1:9

Conversation Starters

- Why did Jesus die on the cross?
- What does it mean to be forgiven and start over?

The SECRET Ingredient of Prayer:

Thank you, Lord, for do-overs. Help my child/children know and feel your grace. May this knowledge give them the desire to follow Your ways. Thank you that my child/children will listen to the conviction of the Holy Spirit, and not live with condemnation and guilt. In Jesus' name, Amen.

Week 3 Observations ~ Thoughts ~ Feelings ~ Prayers

....

....

....

....

....

....

....

....

....

....

....

....

....

....

....

....

....

....

....

WEEK 4

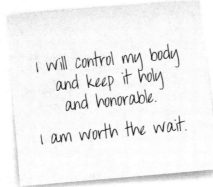

I will control my body
and keep it holy
and honorable.

I am worth the wait.

Scripture:

It is God's will that you should be sanctified: that you should avoid sexual immorality; that each of you should learn to control your own body in a way that is holy and honorable, not in passionate lust like the pagans, who do not know God.

1 Thessalonians 4:3-5

Conversation Starters

- Why is it good to abstain from sex until we are married?
- What are the consequences of not abstaining from sex till we are married?

The SECRET Ingredient of Prayer:

Thank You, my Father, for Your strength when we are weak. Thank You for helping my child/children to refrain from what is not of You. Thank You that Your angels are taking charge over them in tough teenage situations. Thank You that they will remember Your ways and be strengthened in times of weakness. In Jesus' name, Amen.

Week 4 Observations ~ Thoughts ~ Feelings ~ Prayers

....

....

....

....

....

....

....

....

....

....

....

....

....

....

....

....

....

....

Observations ~ Thoughts ~ Feelings ~ Prayers

....

....

....

....

....

....

....

....

....

....

....

....

....

....

....

....

Chapter 5

Love

In my opinion, love is the most misunderstood word in the English language. It's actually not a feeling; it's a lifestyle. Love is a choice. Love is how we behave and treat others. God is love. He demonstrates love in everything He does. God does not allow sin to stand between us and Him; that is why He sent Jesus. What an awesome God! We need to focus on Him, not ourselves.

Take your Expo dry erase pen and write the Post-It sentence on their bathroom mirror. Of course, make sure it's along the top or bottom; we don't want to make it difficult for them to see their pretty little faces.

WEEK 1

> God, You are love. Help me to remember how much You love me no matter what I do.

Scripture:

And so we know and rely on the love God has for us. God is love.
Whoever lives in love lives in God, and God in him.
1 John 4:16

Conversation Starters

- How does God show His love to us?
- What does it mean to love?

The SECRET Ingredient of Prayer:

Dear Lord, You are love. Help my child/children to grasp this. I don't want them to see You as distant. I want them to know that Your sacrifice was priceless. You created them, You love them more than they can even fathom. Help them know You because Your love is not based on our circumstances and that is hard for a teen to understand. You are their Father. Create in them a sense of assurance of Your love. In Jesus' name, Amen.

Week 1 Observations ~ Thoughts ~ Feelings ~ Prayers

....

....

....

....

....

....

....

....

....

....

....

....

....

....

....

....

....

....

....

WEEK 2

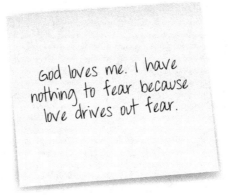

God loves me. I have
nothing to fear because
love drives out fear.

Scripture:

There is no fear in love. But perfect love drives out fear,
because fear has to do with punishment.
The one who fears is not made perfect in love.
1 John 4:18

Conversation Starters

- How does love drive out fear?
- Does God punish us? (God allows things to happen/ but there is an enemy out there)

The SECRET Ingredient of Prayer:

Father in Heaven, thank You that we do not have to fear. Please help me to be an example of this to my children and not scold but explain things to them, not cut them down but encourage them, not lash out but respond in a reasonable manner. Help them to know that You are good and You are good all the time. In Jesus' name, Amen.

Week 2 Observations ~ Thoughts ~ Feelings ~ Prayers

....

....

....

....

....

....

....

....

....

....

....

....

....

....

....

....

....

....

WEEK 3

Lord, thank You for helping my actions show Your love.

Scripture:

Dear children, let us not love with words or tongue but with actions and in truth.

1 John 3:18

Conversation Starters

- Why is it more important to show love through our actions than just words?
- What can you do today to show love?

The SECRET Ingredient of Prayer:

Dear Heavenly Father, thank You that You first loved us through Your actions. You sent Your Son to be the Savior of the world. You truly love us. Help my child/children to show love in their actions, not just their words. In Jesus' name, Amen.

Week 3 Observations ~ Thoughts ~ Feelings ~ Prayers

WEEK 4

> Lord, help me to remember to be patient, kind, not boast, or be proud. Help me to not keep record of who wrongs me. I will love through my actions.

Scripture:

Love is patient, love is kind. It does not envy, it does not boast, it is not proud. It is not rude, it is not self-seeking, it is not easily angered, it keeps no record of wrongs. Love does not delight in evil but rejoices with the truth. It always protects, always trusts, always hopes, always perseveres.

1 Corinthians 13: 4-7

Conversation Starters

- How do we love the unloveable?
- Can we say three nice things about a person we are having a difficult time with?

The SECRET Ingredient of Prayer:

Dear Father, thank You for helping my child/children bring every bad thought into captivity. Help them to be reminded of Your love daily so they in turn can show love. Intercede when they feel the need to boast or feel they are better than others. May they feel good about being a light in this dark world. In Jesus' name, Amen.

Week 4 Observations ~ Thoughts ~ Feelings ~ Prayers

....

....

....

....

....

....

....

....

....

....

....

....

....

....

....

....

....

....

....

Observations ~ Thoughts ~ Feelings ~ Prayers

Chapter 6

Loneliness

Lonely, outcast, depressed, sad, rejected, are just a few words that come to mind for this month's subject. Our teens may feel alone in a crowded school. This is not an easy subject matter because you can console and hug and encourage your teen over and over but they still have so much to learn about their true identity. They need to discipline their thoughts, they need to know their value, they need to know what God says about them, and they need to trust Him. They also need to know that the only one who can fill that void is our Heavenly Father. It's challenging to watch our child/children go through this. The big question is, how are we doing as parents? Are we making them feel valued so that when they do go through times like this, they stay confident?

Put your post-it sentence on the refrigerator. It would be good for the whole family to continue to remind themselves of these truths.

WEEK 1

> I will rejoice in God's love instead of dwelling on my feelings right now.

Scripture:

Be strong and courageous. Do not be afraid or terrified because of them, for the Lord your God goes with you; He will never leave you nor forsake you.
Deuteronomy 31:6

Conversation Starters

- How can we dwell in the assurance of God's love?
- What do you turn to or what do you typically do when you are feeling lonely?

The SECRET Ingredient of Prayer:

Dear Lord, I know we all go through lonely times in our lives but it's especially hard to watch our children go through them. Thank You for comforting them in times of loneliness, thank You for sending them a smile, a pat on the back, and even a friend. And thank You that they will learn that they need to lean on You. In Jesus' name, Amen.

Week 1 Observations ~ Thoughts ~ Feelings ~ Prayers

....

....

....

....

....

....

....

....

....

....

....

....

....

....

....

....

....

....

WEEK 2

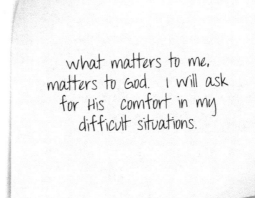

what matters to me,
matters to God. I will ask
for His comfort in my
difficult situations.

Scripture:

Cast all your anxiety on Him because He cares for you.
1 Peter 5:7

Conversation Starters

- Encourage your child to journal during their difficult times. Sometimes it's good to just release your feelings on to paper. Encourage them to pray after writing down their thoughts.

- Maybe at this time they could call an Aunt or Uncle or even a cousin. Maybe have lunch with Grandpa or Grandma.

The SECRET Ingredient of Prayer:

Father, thank You that my child/children are loved. Thank You for helping them to know they are valued. Thank You for sending them Christian friends who will walk alongside them on this journey. May they feel encouraged that life is worth living. In Jesus name. Amen.

Week 2 Observations ~ Thoughts ~ Feelings ~ Prayers

....

....

....

....

....

....

....

....

....

....

....

....

....

....

....

....

....

....

....

WEEK 3

I can never be truly lonely because God is always with me. I also need to remember that other people are feeling the same way or have felt the same way.

Scripture:

Turn to me and be gracious to me, for I am lonely and afflicted.
Psalm 25:16

Conversation Starters

- Talk about being a friend to others who are in need .

- There are teens who walk the halls alone. Even if our teens are not lonely at this time, I always encouraged my children that if they noticed someone who may be lonely or not have any friends to at least smile, or pat them on the back, or say hi. They don't have to hang out with them, but just a nice gesture may be all this person needs to stop their negative thinking.

The SECRET Ingredient of Prayer:

Dear Heavenly Father, thank You that You know what my child/children need. I trust that You will comfort them with a friend, a smile, or hug. I also ask that they, too, learn to notice others who are lonely and initiate a kind gesture of some sort. This world on a whole is lonely and we all need to experience the kindness of Jesus. In Jesus' name, Amen.

Week 3 Observations ~ Thoughts ~ Feelings ~ Prayers

....

....

....

....

....

....

....

....

....

....

....

....

....

....

....

....

....

....

....

WEEK 4

> Lord, You would often withdraw to a place and pray. Encourage me to do the same and I will watch how things transform.

Scripture:

But Jesus often withdrew to lonely places and prayed.
Luke 5:16

Conversation Starters

- Talk about times when Jesus was lonely and how people betrayed Him and what it must have felt like. His Heavenly Father was always there and put the right people in His life.
- Talk about patience and trusting God to bring the right people in their lives. It's ok to wait for something great.

The SECRET Ingredient of Prayer:

Dear Father, thank You that You love my child/children more than I do. Thank You that I do not have to worry about them being lonely. It's only a season. And I know You have great friends for them. And I know You have Your arms around them. In Jesus' name, Amen.

Week 4 Observations ~ Thoughts ~ Feelings ~ Prayers

....

....

....

....

....

....

....

....

....

....

....

....

....

....

....

....

....

Observations ~ Thoughts ~ Feelings ~ Prayers

....

....

....

....

....

....

....

....

....

....

....

....

....

....

....

....

Chapter 7

Blessings

We all want to be blessed. I typed the word blessing into my phone. The first thing that came up was, Dictionary: blessing, God's favor and protection. Yes and indeed we all want to be blessed, feel blessed, live blessed, and be a blessing to others. I want to encourage you to speak out blessings for your teens. And encourage them to speak them out for themselves. God blesses us and He is willing.

Put your post-it sentence on their bedroom door and bathroom doors. It will be nice to encourage them from more than one place.

WEEK 1

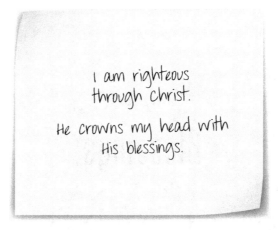

I am righteous through Christ.

He crowns my head with His blessings.

Scripture:

Blessings crown the head of the righteous...
Proverbs 10:6

Conversation Starters

- What does it mean to be blessed?
- Do we realize all our blessings are from God?

The SECRET Ingredient of Prayer:

Dear Lord, thank You for Your many blessings. I pray my child/children realize that all their blessings come from You. Because of what Jesus did on the cross, we are Yours forever and You bring such delight to our lives. I pray they grasp moments of Your goodness and praise You for all of it. I thank You so much for the blessing of my child/children. I am honored to raise them for You. Thank You for being by my side always. In Jesus' name, Amen.

Week 1 Observations ~ Thoughts ~ Feelings ~ Prayers

....

....

....

....

....

....

....

....

....

....

....

....

....

....

....

....

....

....

WEEK 2

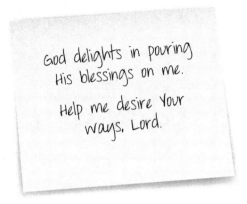

God delights in pouring
His blessings on me.

Help me desire Your
ways, Lord.

Scripture:

"Blessed are those who keep my ways."
Proverbs 8:32

Conversation Starters

- Why does God bless us? Is it just for us?
- What does it mean to desire His ways?

The SECRET Ingredient of Prayer:

Father, thank You that You are so willing to pour out Your blessings on my child/children. Thank You that You will give them the desire to follow Your ways and not the ways of the world. You're such a wonderful Father! May nothing else satisfy us as You do. Thank You that we are blessed. Thank You that we are Yours. In Jesus' name. Amen.

Week 2 Observations ~ Thoughts ~ Feelings ~ Prayers

....

....

....

....

....

....

....

....

....

....

....

....

....

....

....

....

....

....

....

WEEK 3

Thank You, Father, for showers of blessings at the right time and at the right place.

Scripture:

I will make them and the places surrounding my hill a blessing.
I will send down showers in season;
there will be showers of blessing.
Ezekiel 34:26

Conversation Starters

- What kinds of blessings do you desire?
- Why does God desire to bless us?

The SECRET Ingredient of Prayer:

Father, thank You that You are blessing my child/children so that they can be a blessing to others. Thank You for helping them to have the desire to want to bless others. It's better to give than to receive. May they find joy in doing so. In Jesus' name. Amen.

Week 3 Observations ~ Thoughts ~ Feelings ~ Prayers

....

....

....

....

....

....

....

....

....

....

....

....

....

....

....

....

....

....

WEEK 4

> Help me seek and find
> my joy from You,
> Lord.

Scripture:

Taste and see that the Lord is good;
blessed is the man who takes refuge in Him.
Psalm 34:8

Conversation Starters

- What does it mean to taste and see that the Lord is good?
- What does taking refuge in God mean? Do we tend to take refuge in other things like shopping, TV, social media, money, movies etc.?

The SECRET Ingredient of Prayer:

Dear Father, thank You that my child/children will seek and find their joy from You. True joy Lord, not just worldly joy. Thank You that they will trust in Your promises. Help them to take refuge in You and not TV, social media, shopping, movies, and money when they have a challenge or a problem arises. These are escapes, but You have answers, blessings, and favor waiting for them. Keep them close to You. In Jesus' name, Amen.

Week 4 Observations ~ Thoughts ~ Feelings ~ Prayers

....

....

....

....

....

....

....

....

....

....

....

....

....

....

....

....

....

....

....

Observations ~ Thoughts ~ Feelings ~ Prayers

....

....

....

....

....

....

....

....

....

....

....

....

....

....

....

‘
....

....

....

....

Chapter 8

faith

Faith is having confidence in something or someone. In the Bible, it says that faith is *"being sure of what we hope for and certain of what we do not see."* Hebrews 11: 1-2 "Certain of what we do not see." What does that mean? Believing even when it makes no sense to believe. It's because of the trust we place in Jesus. It's the power of God in whom we place our faith. We have to remember that Jesus said, "apart from me you can do nothing." Faith is based on God's ways or His agenda and our trust in Him. I love that faith is based on God's promises because, if God promises it, then it will come to pass. Our faith helps us overcome our sin, worry, doubt, and our trials. Let us help our kids have childlike faith.

Put your post-it messages on their dresser, either on the mirror or on top somewhere.

WEEK 1

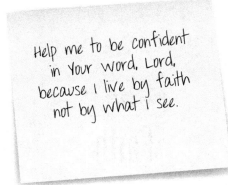

Help me to be confident in Your word, Lord, because I live by faith not by what I see.

Scripture:

We live by faith not by sight.
2 Corinthians 5:7

Conversation Starters

- What does it mean to live by faith and not by sight?
- Explain that it takes tremendous courage and strength to walk by faith. God will reveal things as we walk in obedience. Our teens need to give up control to God. At times, they will be misunderstood; but there are great rewards and blessings along the journey.

The SECRET Ingredient of Prayer:

Lord, thank You so much for the Bible. Thank You for giving my child/ children courage to stand up for what they believe and confidence in You to trust every word You have given us. Lead my family to pastors and youth leaders who speak truth and who have a personal relationship with You and not religion. In Jesus' name, Amen.

Week 1 Observations ~ Thoughts ~ Feelings ~ Prayers

....

....

....

....

....

....

....

....

....

....

....

....

....

....

....

....

....

....

WEEK 2

Father, encourage me to hear sermons and open up my Bible to gain more wisdom from You.

This will increase my faith.

Scripture:

Consequently, faith comes from hearing the message, and the message is heard through the word about Christ.

Romans 10:17

Conversation Starters

- Why will hearing the word increase our faith?
- Is hearing the Word of God once a week enough?

The SECRET Ingredient of Prayer:

Father in Heaven, thank You that we do not have to do this on our own. I trust that You are speaking to my child/children daily. I thank You that I do not have to worry. I know that as for me and my house, we will follow You! In Jesus' name, Amen.

Week 2 Observations ~ Thoughts ~ Feelings ~ Prayers

....

....

....

....

....

....

....

....

....

....

....

....

....

....

....

....

....

....

WEEK 3

> Father, thank You for putting great christian leaders and christian friends in my life. We need to encourage one another.

Scripture:

...that is, that you and I may be mutually encouraged by each other's faith.

Romans 1:12

Conversation Starters

- Does it matter who we surround ourselves with?
- Why is it good to encourage each other in our faith walk?

The SECRET Ingredient of Prayer:

Dear Heavenly Father, thank You that not only do You encourage my child/children, but You will surround them with Christian leaders and friends who will do the same. I pray that my child/children will also encourage others in their faith and be a good example of Jesus to them. In Jesus' name, Amen.

Week 3 Observations ~ Thoughts ~ Feelings ~ Prayers

....

....

....

....

....

....

....

....

....

....

....

....

....

....

....

....

....

....

WEEK 4

> Faith is being sure of what I hope for and certain of what I do not see. I have hope in Your word, Father. Help me to have certainty in Your promises for my life.

Scripture:

Now faith is confidence in what we hope for and assurance about what we do not see.

Hebrews 11:1

Conversation Starters

- What does it mean to be sure of what we hope for and certain of what we do not see?
- Tell your teens to go through the Bible and find God's promises for their life and claim them for themselves.

The SECRET Ingredient of Prayer:

Dear Father, thank You for giving my child/children the desire to learn Your promises. Let them experience Your awesomeness in their lives. Help them to remember that You have been faithful in many ways and that You are working on their behalf. I know You love them more than I can even fathom. Help me to release them into Your hands. In Jesus' name, Amen.

Week 4 Observations ~ Thoughts ~ Feelings ~ Prayers

....

....

....

....

....

....

....

....

....

....

....

....

....

....

....

....

....

....

....

Observations ~ Thoughts ~ Feelings ~ Prayers

....

....

....

....

....

....

....

....

....

....

....

....

....

....

....

....

....

....

Chapter 9
Bitterness & Forgiveness

This month's subjects are big ones. For me, they are the most important. The battlefield of the mind is huge. It contributes to so much of who we are, how we act, the health of our mind, soul, and body. Teaching forgiveness to kids at a young age is extremely important. At times, I would hear my kids say, "I hate so and so, I hate that teacher, I hate that team, I hate that coach." It may not be true hate, but I would immediately say, "You don't hate anyone." In response they would say, "Yes I do." After their response, I instructed them on what happens when we hate someone and the fact that when we hate, we allow that person, in a way, to rent space in our minds. I've been through this personally. It took me a long time to finally realize that my mind was controlling me instead of me controlling my mind. The spiraling of my health started in my mind. Bitterness was the biggest contributor which led to unforgiveness. Let's help our kids renew their minds. With a lot of love, determination, and prayer, we can help them. It's discipline. They can learn to control their thoughts.

I recommend putting sticky notes on the refrigerator and on doors to their bedrooms. It's a post-it that would be good to be seen in many parts of the home.

WEEK 1

I am not perfect and neither are those who hurt me. Because God has forgiven me, I, too, will forgive others.

Scripture:

And forgive us our debts, as we also have forgiven our debtors. And lead us not into temptation, but deliver us from the evil one. For if you forgive other people when they sin against you, your heavenly Father will also forgive you. But if you do not forgive others their sins, your Father will not forgive your sins.

Matthew 6:12-15

Conversation Starters

- Do you feel God truly forgives you?
- Why do we feel our sins are ok to be forgiven but that the sins of others who sin against us don't deserve to be forgiven?

The SECRET Ingredient of Prayer:

Dear Lord, thank You for helping my child/children hold firmly to what Jesus did on the cross for them. You have totally forgiven us. And although it is hard, please give them the desire to forgive others. Remind them of what You have done for us so that they can release others from that strong grip. In Jesus' name, Amen.

Week 1 Observations ~ Thoughts ~ Feelings ~ Prayers

WEEK 2

> I will not allow bitterness to take root in my heart.

Scripture:

See to it that no one misses the grace of God and that no bitter root grows up to cause trouble and defile many.

Hebrews 12:15

Conversation Starters

- What does it mean to take root?
- What are the consequences of holding onto unforgiveness?

The SECRET Ingredient of Prayer:

Father in Heaven, thank You that bitterness will not take root in my child/children's hearts. I don't want my child/children feeling distant from You because they carry around anger. This is one of the hardest things to do and I step in and pray for them to be released from this. Nothing formed against them will prosper. Bitterness is poison and it is not of You. Set them free. In Jesus' name, Amen.

Week 2 Observations ~ Thoughts ~ Feelings ~ Prayers

....

....

....

....

....

....

....

....

....

....

....

....

....

....

....

....

....

....

WEEK 3

I will not allow the enemy to get into my head. He is trying to destroy me.
I want to get rid of all bitterness, rage, and anger.

Thank You, Lord, for helping me to forgive because I can't do it on my own.

Scripture:

Get rid of all bitterness, rage and anger, brawling and slander, along with every form of malice. Be kind and compassionate to one another, forgiving each other, just as in Christ God forgave you.
Ephesians 4:31-32

Conversation Starters

- What does the devil do to get inside your head?
- Why does he want you angry, bitter, and mad?

The SECRET Ingredient of Prayer:

Dear Heavenly Father, the devil wants to destroy us but You already said that we are victorious. Bitterness will only bring my child/children down. You have already won the war on evil. Let kindness and compassion and forgiveness take root in my child/children's hearts. Let them live free. In Jesus' name, Amen.

Week 3 Observations ~ Thoughts ~ Feelings ~ Prayers

WEEK 4

Lord, I want to trust that you will fight for me and help me let the offense or hurt go.

Scripture:

Do not repay evil with evil or insult with insult.
On the contrary, repay evil with blessing, because to this you were
called so that you may inherit a blessing.

1 Peter 3:9

Conversation Starters

- Jeremiah 17: 7-8 says…"But blessed is the one who trusts in the Lord, whose confidence is in Him." Repaying evil with evil means we do not trust God to take care of the circumstance. What does it mean to have God take care of the situation?

- Explain how learning to let go and trust God to handle those who have hurt us brings freedom to our minds.

The SECRET Ingredient of Prayer:

Thank You again, Father, for helping my child/children bring every bad thought into captivity and setting them free from bitterness in their spirit. They can win the battle by walking away and controlling their minds to think on good. They will not rent space in their head for hate. Please help them to see at least an ounce of good in all people who have hurt them or who have hurt people they love. In Jesus' name, Amen.

Week 4 Observations ~ Thoughts ~ Feelings ~ Prayers

....

....

....

....

....

....

....

....

....

....

....

....

....

....

....

....

....

....

....

Observations ~ Thoughts ~ Feelings ~ Prayers

....
....
....
....
....
....
....
....
....
....
....
....
....
....
....
....
....
....
....

Chapter 10
Uncertainty About The Future

Uncertainty about the future is something we all tend to think about from time to time. I mean, realistically, none of us know what the future holds. But God does. And He also gives us what we need to accomplish His purpose. It's easy to lose hope.

Let's remind our teen(s) that God is certain about our future. And let's encourage them to trust Him in all things. Place your sticky note on their headboard of their bed.

WEEK 1

> I acknowledge that God has me
> right where I am for a reason.
> He is directing my steps.

Scripture:

"For I know the plans I have for you," declares the Lord,
"plans to prosper you and not to harm you,
plans to give you hope and a future."
Jeremiah 29:11

Conversation Starters

- What does it mean when I say, "God is in control, not your circumstances?"
- Do you know God has good things in store for you?

The SECRET Ingredient of Prayer:

Dear Heavenly Father, I thank You that You are in control of things going on around us. You see my children and You know their journey. Thank You for making their crooked paths straight. I thank You that You are directing their steps right now as I pray. In Jesus' name, Amen.

Week 1 Observations ~ Thoughts ~ Feelings ~ Prayers

....

....

....

....

....

....

....

....

....

....

....

....

....

....

....

....

....

....

WEEK 2

God, I know You can do
what men cannot do.
You are my provider.

Scripture:

You open your hand and satisfy the desires of every living thing.
Psalm 145:16

Conversation Starters

- How has God been our provider?
- How is God our source?

The SECRET Ingredient of Prayer:

Dear Heavenly Father, I thank You that You are my family's source and You so wonderfully provide for us. I thank You that my son/daughter will acknowledge this truth. In Jesus' name, Amen.

Week 2 Observations ~ Thoughts ~ Feelings ~ Prayers

....

....

....

....

....

....

....

....

....

....

....

....

....

....

....

....

....

....

WEEK 3

I have nothing to stand on except God's word. I will start acting as though God's word is true, being positive and hopeful about my situation. I am putting actions behind my faith. This gets God's attention.

Scripture:

All your words are true; all your righteous laws are eternal.
Psalm 119:160

Conversation Starters

- How can we believe God's Word in times of trouble?
- If the season of life I am in right now looks miserable, how can I count on God to change it around?

The SECRET Ingredient of Prayer:

Dear Heavenly Father, sometimes it is hard to believe Your Word when we are down. Please give my son/daughter peace in this time of uncertainty. Thank You that these hard circumstances are only learning opportunities and my child/children will persevere and come out strong. In Jesus' name, Amen.

Week 3 Observations ~ Thoughts ~ Feelings ~ Prayers

WEEK 4

> God would not have put the desires and dreams in my heart if He had not intended to give me everything I will need to fulfill it.

Scripture:

Take delight in the Lord,
and He will give you the desires of your heart.

Psalm 37:4

Conversation Starters

- What talents or gifts has God given me?
- What can I do to strengthen my gifts?

The SECRET Ingredient of Prayer:

Dear Heavenly Father, I thank You so much for the gifts and talents You have given my son/daughter. Thank You that You will renew their mind to focus on all You have for them. Thank You that You will continue to guide him/her in the direction You have planned. If he/she gets off track, I trust that You will redirect him/her in Your loving ways. In Jesus' name I pray, Amen.

Week 4 Observations ~ Thoughts ~ Feelings ~ Prayers

....

....

....

....

....

....

....

....

....

....

....

....

....

....

....

....

....

Observations ~ Thoughts ~ Feelings ~ Prayers

....

....

....

....

....

....

....

....

....

....

....

....

....

....

....

....

....

....

Uncertainty About The Future   133

Chapter 11
Your Worth

We are very valuable to God. Some of our children may not feel valued by their parents, friends, teachers, or coaches. So, why would they feel valued by God? I have included four scriptures to help them hear what God has to say about them. If we could just get them to focus on God's Word and help them hear it and hear it and hear it, I'm hoping that when they do feel unvalued, they will know that the King of Kings, and the Lord of Lords, and their Abba Father in heaven is crazy over them. There are so many sermons about what we need to do. God just wants his children to know He adores them and that He wants a relationship with them. Everything else is secondary.

WEEK 1

> I am a child of God!
> The creator of the earth
> calls me HIS!

Scripture:

See what great love the Father has lavished on us, that we should be called children of God! And that is what we are!

1 John 3:1

Conversation Starters

- What does it mean to be called a child of God?
- We need to ponder on the fact that the God of heaven and earth has chosen us. When we know He chose us, that means He has us here for a reason. Why do you think God has chosen you?

The SECRET Ingredient of Prayer:

Dear Heavenly Father, I thank You that You value my child/children and call them Yours. I thank You that my child/children will know that they are crowned with favor and victory and that they will know how unique and special they are in Your eyes. Help them to have the confidence they need so they don't have low self-esteem whether they bring it on themselves or someone has said something to hurt them. In Jesus' name, Amen.

Week 1 Observations ~ Thoughts ~ Feelings ~ Prayers

....

....

....

....

....

....

....

....

....

....

....

....

....

....

....

....

....

WEEK 2

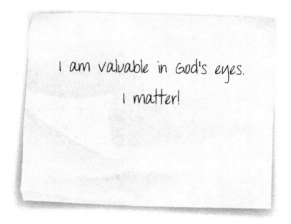

I am valuable in God's eyes.
I matter!

Scripture:

*Consider the ravens: They do not sow or reap, they have no storeroom
or barn; yet God feeds them.
And how much more valuable you are than birds!*
Luke 12:24

Conversation Starters

- How do we know we are not average or ordinary?
- What people/things are valuable to us? Why?

The SECRET Ingredient of Prayer:

Dear Heavenly Father, I thank You that my child/children are not average or ordinary. In Your timing, may they excel in all that You have created them for. Along the way, inspire, encourage, and protect them. I thank You that my son/daughter will acknowledge this truth. In Jesus' name, Amen.

Week 2 Observations ~ Thoughts ~ Feelings ~ Prayers

....

....

....

....

....

....

....

....

....

....

....

....

....

....

....

....

....

....

WEEK 3

> The Lord takes
> delight in me.
>
> He rejoices over the fact
> that I am His!

Scripture:

The Lord your God is with you, the Mighty Warrior who saves.
He will take great delight in you; in his love he will no longer rebuke
you, but will rejoice over you with singing.
Zephaniah 3:17

Conversation Starters

- How can we believe God's Word when we don't feel valuable?
- Talk about changing your mindset. It takes discipline.

The SECRET Ingredient of Prayer:

Dear Heavenly Father, sometimes it is hard to believe that we are valuable. The people around my child/children may be saying negative things, or our kids may experience disappointments. Thank You that Your leading of the Holy Spirit will confirm in my children their value. Thank You that You will bring others into their lives that will confirm this as well. In Jesus' name I pray, Amen.

Week 3 Observations ~ Thoughts ~ Feelings ~ Prayers

WEEK 4

> God is full of compassion for me.
> He protects and saves me.

Scripture:

The Lord is gracious and righteous; our God is full of compassion. The Lord protects the simple-hearted ;
when I was in great need, He saved me.

Psalm 116: 5-6

Conversation Starters

- Why does God continue to be full of compassion for us even when we continue to do wrong?

- Meditate on the fact that God is compassionate toward us and protects us and saves us. Doesn't that in itself prove how valuable we are?

The SECRET Ingredient of Prayer:

Dear Heavenly Father, I thank You so much that we are righteous through Christ. You value us so much that You sent Jesus. Thank You for helping my child/children realize this. Thank You for sparks of excitement in their lives that brings out their inner joy of knowing that they are Yours and that they are wonderfully and perfectly made in Your image. In Jesus' name, Amen.

Week 4 Observations ~ Thoughts ~ Feelings ~ Prayers

....

....

....

....

....

....

....

....

....

....

....

....

....

....

....

....

....

....

Observations ~ Thoughts ~ Feelings ~ Prayers

....

....

....

....

....

....

....

....

....

....

....

....

....

....

....

....

....

....

....

Chapter 12

Healing

I want everyone to get this chapter. The Lord is our Alpha and our Omega. He is in full control. What He speaks in the beginning will come through in the end. But it takes our faith to move mountains. It takes our words to proclaim His promises over our lives. Do not let your child/children compare themselves to other kids. I don't know what other people believe. I do not know what is in their hearts about truth. We can't compare our situations to others. Just because someone else died of a certain disease does not mean we are going to. It's important to look at the scriptures, have hope, and believe that God's word trumps the devil. It doesn't mean that bad things won't come our way; but, if they do, what is our attitude? Are we still believing on, worshiping and thanking Him for the passing of the negative circumstances from our lives? I've personally learned that when I feel a pain, I tell the devil he is a liar and I focus on Jesus. I also ask for wisdom for the situation, knowing in my heart that He will take care of it. If I worry, then I seem to get worse. Rest in Jesus. And help your child/children to do so as well.

WEEK 1

My God forgives all my sins and heals all my diseases.

He takes me from trouble and lifts me up with His love and grace.

Scripture:

Praise the Lord, O my soul, and forget not all his benefits- who forgives all your sins and heals all your diseases, who redeems your life from the pit and crowns you with love and compassion.

Psalm 103:2-4

Conversation Starters

- We are told that God forgives all our sins and heals all our diseases. Explain how it is important to apologize to God for our sins. Share with your child/children that sins lead to toxic build-up in our bodies. God does not want us living with condemnation. If we internalize the love and forgiveness from our Heavenly Father, we can live free and our bodies will heal.

- How do we believe this truth with so many bad reports on the news? Let's teach our child/children to study truth and turn off the TV.

The SECRET Ingredient of Prayer:

Dear Heavenly Father, I thank You so much for my child/children. I ask in Jesus' name that all that is not of You be removed from their bodies. Thank You for teaching my child/children that You have forgiven them of all their sins. Help them to not feel condemned. Condemnation kills. Set my child/children free and allow healing to take over in their minds and in their bodies. In Jesus' name, Amen.

Week 1 Observations ~ Thoughts ~ Feelings ~ Prayers

....

....

....

....

....

....

....

....

....

....

....

....

....

....

....

....

....

....

WEEK 2

> Lord, help me to avoid all
> evil and be in awe of You.
> This will bring health to
> my whole body.

Scripture:

Do not be wise in your own eyes;
fear the Lord and shun evil. This will bring
health to your body and nourishment to your bones.
Proverbs 3:7-8

Conversation Starters

- Talk to your child about how God does not want them thinking of the "what if's". He wants them envisioning themselves healthy and whole.

- Besides prayer and speaking God's Word over our lives, we should also pray for wisdom on what God wants us to change so we can become healthier. It could be our attitudes, changing our hearts, minds, or to change a habit.

The SECRET Ingredient of Prayer:

Dear Father, I know You are on this journey with my child/children. I know You use circumstances to help change us. Give my child/children wisdom to change whatever it is they need to do differently, whether it's to let go of a past or recent hurt, or to eat better or exercise, or maybe it's to avoid confrontation. Whatever it is, thank You for Your knowledge in this situation. In Jesus' name, Amen.

Week 2 Observations ~ Thoughts ~ Feelings ~ Prayers

....

....

....

....

....

....

....

....

....

....

....

....

....

....

....

....

....

WEEK 3

why do I doubt Your word? Help me realize all You did for me on the cross. You set me free from my offenses, bad behavior, and healed my spirit, body, and soul. when my mind is on Jesus, my mind, body, and spirit are set free.

Scripture:

But he was pierced for our transgressions,
he was crushed for our iniquities; the punishment that brought us
peace was upon him, and by his wounds we are healed.

Isaiah 53:5

Conversation Starters

- Why is the cross the perfect remedy for us?
- Since Jesus redeemed us from the curse of the law on the cross, and sickness is included in the curse, then surely He redeemed us from sickness and disease.

The SECRET Ingredient of Prayer:

Father God, You alone are our Jehovah-Rapha, our Great physician. Help our children to desire Your ways, search out answers from Your Word, and to be free from bondage. In doing so, they will live the abundant, free life You died to give them. Circumstances will come, but teach them how to deal with them Your way so they stay healthy in their mind, soul, and body. In Jesus' name, Amen.

Week 3 Observations ~ Thoughts ~ Feelings ~ Prayers

....

....

....

....

....

....

....

....

....

....

....

....

....

....

....

....

....

....

....

WEEK 4

Lord show me Your ways, help me focus on Your word for it gives me life and health.

Scripture:

My son, pay attention to what I say; turn your ear to my words. Do not let them out of your sight, keep them within your heart; for they are life to those who find them and health to one's whole body.

Proverbs 4:20-22

Conversation Starters

- Why does God ask us to pay attention to His Words and to not let them depart from us?

- Share a time when you wish you would have followed God's Word instead of your own desires. What happened? What was the outcome?

The SECRET Ingredient of Prayer:

Dear Heavenly Father, help my child/children to receive Your love and to have faith in Your perfect Word. Let them watch Your faithfulness unfold. I believe Your favor is on their life and You will give them the patience for Your timing in all areas of their life. Thank You for walking with them and never leaving them. In Jesus' name, Amen.

Week 4 Observations ~ Thoughts ~ Feelings ~ Prayers

....

....

....

....

....

....

....

....

....

....

....

....

....

....

....

....

....

....

Observations ~ Thoughts ~ Feelings ~ Prayers

Getting It to Stick

About the Author

Debbie Bailey is a mother of four and raising a foster-daughter. She has a passion for God's word and His children. She leads a women's Bible study in her home where she has long listened carefully to the concerns of many mothers for their children. A long-time Sunday school teacher at Cherry Hills Community Church, where she also served on the church's missions committee and was active in collecting funds and needed supplies for local Pregnancy Centers. Debbie co-wrote *The Daughters Of Our King*, (published for in-church use) a book for teenage girls, about God and His truths on abstinence, eating disorders, dating, drugs, suicide, etc. She has taught classes to moms and teenage girls based on this book. Debbie and her husband and children live in Lone Tree, Colorado where they attend Jubilee Community Church.

Connect with Debbie on social media:

 @ DebRBailey    @debbierbailey

CPSIA information can be obtained
at www.ICGtesting.com
Printed in the USA
LVHW050052120419
613928LV00007B/66/P